CORVETTE STINGRAY

1963-1967

Bob Ackerson

CONTENTS

Foulis

Haynes

ISBN 0 85429 432 5

A FOULIS Motoring Book

First published 1984

© **Haynes Publishing Group**

Published by:
Haynes Publishing Group
Sparkford, Yeovil,
Somerset BA22 7JJ

Distributed in USA by:
Haynes Publications Inc.
861 Lawrence Drive, Newbury Park,
California 91320, USA

Editor: Rod Grainger
Dust jacket design: Rowland Smith
Page Layout: Peter Kay
Road tests: Courtesy of Autosport
and Sports Car Graphic
Printed in England by: J.H.Haynes
& Co. Ltd

Further titles in this series will be published at
regular intervals. For information on new titles
please contact your bookseller or write to the
publisher.

FOREWORD

The Corvette, now into its fourth decade of production, has become a world class automobile. The latest version when compared to contemporary Porsche and Ferrari models invariably proves to be fully worthy of such an exercise. This degree of acceptance has been, in the view of many Corvette owners, long overdue. Although the first Corvettes had some major shortcomings, they were true sports cars and for over 30 years every Corvette that has followed has been a sports car. There aren't many automobiles currently in production that can claim a similar heritage. But the Corvette, in the eyes of its unyielding critics, lacked the proper breeding it needed to be accepted as a thoroughbred sports car. It was built by a manufacturer better known for oversized Impalas than for high performance two-seaters.

But such foolishness ignored the obvious. The Corvette appeared at the right time and place. America in the early fifties was ready for the revival of the sports car and as luck would have it, the Corvette, after its first few years of production represented what most American sports car owners wanted. Their number one desire was performance, real performance that needed no excuses or alibis. The Corvette had awesome acceleration, great top speed and decent handling, all at a reasonable price.

By 1963, when the first Sting Ray model appeared, the Corvette name was known worldwide; it was already an automobile with a distinct character, that was unique amongst contemporary sports cars. The Sting Ray not only lived up to this reputation but greatly enhanced it. On every point it was superior to its predecessors and if the Cobra took away some of its road racing lustre, it remained near the top of any list of the world's great sports cars.

Today Corvettes of the 1963-67 era are held in great esteem. Although produced in relatively large numbers their desirability has made for dramatic price increases. Furthermore, their owners embrace them with an enthusiasm that no other modern American automobile seems able to elicit. Thus the quality of restored models steadily increases and the mass of technical and historical data about them continues to expand.

From the ranks of the Corvette faithful came the cars and owners who contributed to this *Super Profile* in many valuable ways. Car owners Bill Lado, Gary Enck, Tony Sofia, Bob Philopulous, Mike Duczak, Ken Mennella, Linda and Mike Strunk, and John Warunek, not only offered their cars for photographic purposes but also freely gave much valuable information. The research conducted by the National Corvette Restorers Society was also a vital source of accurate technical data. Charles Jordan of GM Design generously provided photos of pre-production Corvettes. Special thanks go to Hank Briscoe of the Glen Region Corvette Club who directed the author to owners of some of the finest surviving examples of the 1963-67 Corvette.

Bob Ackerson

H. 12355

HISTORY

For most of its history Chevrolet has produced automobiles that are anything but exciting. Reliability, economy and low initial maintenance costs were qualities that had enabled Chevrolet, since 1936, to outsell its archrival Ford and thus become the most popular marque in the world. But while this formula for success kept Chevrolet in the forefront during the immediate postwar years, there were plenty of signs that its days were numbered. In the early fifties, Ford, having totally recovered from the damage wrought by the final years of Henry Ford's reign, was fully capable of once again offering serious competition to Chevrolet. This challenge would take place in an environment where performance and styling would be of paramount importance. Ever since 1948, when Cadillac's tail-finned models had been introduced, American styling had steadily become more and more daring. This move to a more exciting (if on more than one occasion somewhat overdone!) appearance was matched by an equally important revolution under the hood. Cadillac had been first, followed closely by Oldsmobile, with overhead valve V8 engines that along with Chrysler's hemi-head V8 of 1951 found their way into virtually every type of automobile competition in existence.

This age of high performance was paralleled by a revival of American interest in sports cars. Stimulated by the early post war MGTC and driven to a fever pitch by the considerably more potent Jaguar XK120 and early Porsches, the sports car movement in the U.S. had by 1951 reached a level that Detroit ignored at its own peril. Nothing of this sort was taking place at General Motors. The Company's styling chief Harley Earl, who had years earlier in 1926 established himself at General Motors with a design for the 1927 LaSalle that successfully applied European styling concepts to an American mass-produced automobile, saw to that. Convinced that a fairly profitable market existed for a low-priced American-built two-seater, Earl directed a group of his stylists in June 1951 to design such an automobile. General Motors had a well defined procedure by which proposals such as this were evaluated by various corporate committees. Earl virtually guaranteed this car's blessing by the all-important policy committee by keeping certain key officials informed of its development.

From this point the sequence of events that was to convert Earl's low priced two-seater into the Chevrolet Corvette rapidly fell into place. Ed Cole who had earlier not only been deeply involved in the development of Cadillac's new V8 but had also assisted Briggs Cunningham in preparing his team of two Cadillacs for the 1950 Le Mans race became Chevrolet's number one engineer in early 1952. Charged by his superiors to revitalize Chevrolet's staid image with some new products (that included a V8 engine) Cole moved quickly to make certain that the plaster mock-up of Earl's two-seater carried a Chevrolet bow tie. Thus when the 1953 General Motors Motorama show opened on January 17 at the Waldorf-Astoria in New York City the manifestation of Earl's vision was supported by a Chevrolet chassis and powered by a Chevrolet engine. This "Dream Car" was identified as the Corvette: a name which Chevrolet explained had previously been used to identify "the trim, fleet naval vessel that performed heroic escort and patrol duties in World War II". Chevrolet estimated that some four million people saw the Corvette as it toured the country.

Chevrolet wasn't the only American manufacturer to produce a postwar two-seater sports car. Nash-Kelvinator, parent to the Anglo-American Nash-Healey and Kaiser-Frazer Companies, began output of its Kaiser-Darrin in December 1953. An even earlier American entry into the sports car field was the Crosley Hotshot/Super Sport. However Chevrolet moved very rapidly to capitalize on the public's extremely positive response to the Corvette. A short, six car, assembly line was established in what had served as Chevrolet's Customer Delivery Garage in Flint, Michigan, and there the first Corvette was completed on June 30, 1953. After the initial batch of 300 Corvettes were built production was transferred to St. Louis where it remained until July 1981. Currently Corvettes are built at Bowling Green, Kentucky.

Chevrolet had easily beaten Ford to the starting grid in the race to be first with an American two-seater (the Ford Thunderbird's production didn't begin until September 1954) but this advantage proved of little importance since the Thunderbird was soon outselling the Corvette by a huge margin. In 1955 Thunderbird production totalled 16,155. Only 4,640 Corvettes were built from 1953 through 1955. Chevrolet obviously had erred on many key points. The Corvette's fibreglass body was a novelty and probably a plus factor, but no one was enthused about its archaic side curtains and few sports car drivers could comprehend the logic of its standard transmission being the two-speed Powerglide automatic. Although the Corvette's 6-cylinder,

235 cubic inch, 150 horsepower engine delivered the appropriate exhaust note and good (zero to 60mph in approximately 11 seconds) acceleration, it was still a six-cylinder engine. With ohv V8s such as the Thunderbird's in vogue, it soon became apparent that the Corvette, if it was to survive, needed a similar engine.

As events soon made evident, the Corvette, beginning in 1955, not only received an engine that enabled it to match the Thunderbird on this important selling point, but also a power unit which possessed the elements of greatness in the proper proportions to earn recognition as one of the outstanding American engines of all time.

Turn around time for the Corvette was the 1956 model year. The positive impact of Zora Arkus-Duntov (who had joined General Motors in May 1953) upon the Corvette's design, plus a major redesign of the Corvette made this a vintage year for the model. A three-speed manual gearbox was available (only a very few had been installed on the 1955 Corvettes), handsome new styling was introduced and all Corvettes were V8-powered. The standard 265cid engine developed 210hp and with dual 4-barrel carburetors its output was increased to 225 horsepower. For competition purposes a special Duntov-designed cam was available which provided approximately 240hp at 5800rpm.

In SCCA competition the Corvette quickly proved not only to be the master of the Jaguar XK140 but with increasing frequency it demonstrated an ability to out-race the Mercedes-Benz 300SL.

The following year with its fuel-injected engine developing 283hp and a fully synchronized four-speed gear box available, the Corvette became one of the world's fastest production sports cars. Although some styling regresses accompanied the introduction of dual headlights on the 1958 model, the Corvette was, by 1962, a very

attractive automobile. Its engine, now expanded to 327 cubic inches and with fuel-injection, produced 360 horsepower: sufficient to propel Corvette to the SCCA's Class A production national championship.

However, time had caught up with the Corvette's suspension which by 1962 was nearly a decade old. Thus, while the production Corvette was steadily growing in popularity, work on its replacement was under way.

Although the development of the new Corvette, as the XP-720, began in October 1959, its genesis was traceable back to a much earlier date. As early as December 1957 Zora Arkus-Duntov had established a set of design priorities that the 1963 Sting Ray would fulfil in magnificent fashion. Key areas Duntov highlighted for future introduction included both more comfortable seating for its occupants and increased luggage space. Its ride and handling needed to be significantly updated and while the Corvette in its 1958 form with up to 290hp and four-speed transmission was capable of a zero to 60mph time of less than six seconds and a 130+mph top speed, Duntov envisioned a Corvette capable of even greater performance.

While Duntov was musing over these specifics major developments were taking place at GM Styling, developments that were to ensure that the 1963 Corvette would have styling every bit as sensational as its performance. On December 1, 1958 William L. Mitchell succeeded Harley Earl as General Motors' vice-president in charge of styling and while this change marked the end of one era of styling philosophy and the start of another, it also meant that the man with the most to say about the Corvette's form continued to be a strong proponent of sports cars. Mitchell had, in the mid-thirties, joined the Automobile Racing Club of America which as a forerunner of the Sports

Car Club of America represented the roots from which the American postwar sports car movement grew.

The early Corvettes with their standard two-speed Powerglide transmissions and 150hp, six-cylinder engines were not competitive in sports car racing. However, the arrival of a V8 engine, four-speed all-synchromesh transmission and fuel-injection transformed the Corvette from a pussycat to a tiger. By 1956 not only was it regarded as one of the world's outstanding production sports cars but for a time it appeared likely that a competition version would cross the Atlantic to challenge the European factory teams at Le Mans. After a four car Corvette team placed two cars in 9th and 15th position at Sebring in 1956 a crash programme was undertaken that resulted in a single SS Corvette appearing on the grid for the 1957 Sebring Twelve Hours. Its run for glory that day was limited to just 23 laps, but the suspension ills leading to its premature retirement could not overshadow its potential as a serious competitor in international competition. The door was shut for all time on the SS Corvette's development when Chevrolet was forced to terminate its racing programme under the terms of the June 1957 AMA anti-performance edict. However, great cars die hard and in April 1959 a left-over chassis from the SS programme, endowed with an exciting fibreglass body, made its racing debut at the Marlboro Raceway in the state of Maryland. Its owner was none other than William Mitchell and the born again SS was now known as the Sting Ray. Although the Sting Ray's appearance was startling to race goers, it was familiar to a group of GM stylists who during the previous year had completed work on a dramatic new Corvette that was to have been marketed in 1960. This Q-Corvette would have featured a rear transaxle and a lightweight fastback coupe body.

The Sting Ray was of course a roadster but its peaked front and rear fenders, dramatic side body crease and forward-protruding hood line were all derived from the Q-Corvette.

After its two-season racing career (which included a Class C-Modified championship) ended, the Sting Ray went on tour as a show car. At the same time, a production counterpart Sting Ray was well along on the road to completion. While Mitchell's Sting Ray was the direct antecedent of the new Corvette's styling, its engineering predecessor was the experimental, rear-engined CERV-1 vehicle. Although the effort by Duntov to have the 1963 Corvette adopt a rear-engine format was unsuccessful, its improved front-rear weight distribution (which went from 51%-front, 49% rear to 47%-front, 53%-rear) and considerably lower (16.5 inches) centre of gravity, were examples of the CERV-1 influence. The XP-720 adopted a perimeter type chassis frame with box section side rails and five cross-members in place of the X-member version that had remained essentially unchanged from 1953 through 1962.

The XP-720 Corvette's front suspension was a conventional combination of unequal length wishbones, tubular shocks mounted concentrically within coil springs, spherical joints and a forward-mounted stabilizer bar. Considerably more startling was the format Chevrolet adopted for the Corvette's independent rear suspension. A nine leaf, transversely positioned spring, mounted to a fixed differential carrier controlled movement in the vertical plane. Lateral control was provided by a three-link arrangement consisting of the wheel driveshaft, camber control strut rod and the trailing wheel spindle support arm. Corvette engineers had as two of their objectives of this new suspension an improved ride and a higher level of handling competence and on

both points they scored major successes. Whereas the rear suspension of the 1962 Corvette had 301 pounds of unsprung weight, its replacement had one-third less at just 200 pounds.

The coupe version of the XP-720 (whose external trunk lid was eliminated from the production model due to its cost) was completed prior to the designing of its convertible running mate with optional, detachable hardtop. Although the coupe with its fastback roofline and neo-classic boat-tail represented a new design format for the Corvette, there was a slim possibility for a time that its impact and indeed the Corvette's hard won image would be seriously diluted by a proposal from Chevrolet general manager Ed Cole that a 4-place version be considered. Fortunately for all involved, this project did not progress beyond a full-sized mock-up. Instead the Corvette's design philosophy remained intact as exemplified by the results of performance tests conducted at General Motors' 5 mile Milford, Michigan test track. Equipped with 3.08:1 rear axle, non-standard 8.20 x 15 tires and the 360hp fuel-injected engine a Sting Ray coupe reached a maximum speed of 161mph. Its roadster counterpart peaked at 156mph.

Work to retool the St. Louis, Missouri Corvette assembly plant for the new Sting Ray model began early in the spring of 1963. This was no small undertaking since most fixtures and equipment had to be replaced. Operation of all assembly units conformed to a $\frac{1}{16}$inch tolerance and once in place a temporary assembly line began a pilot production run of 25 Corvettes. These cars were later used for press and public showings.

All fibreglass body panels for the 1963 Corvette were completely new with the largest being the floor panel. Other major components included the rear deck, top, rear quarter panels, door sections and the inner and outer fender units.

Both the coupe and convertible bodies had their passenger compartment framed within a steel structure dubbed the "birdcage" by Chevrolet. When intended for a convertible this unit received added sill and lock pillar reinforcements. Before the birdcage was joined to the floor panels, many sub-assemblies of smaller fibreglass units were completed. Prior to the commencement of the body painting process all body seams were finished to a smooth surface (these efforts notwithstanding, poor body quality was a major criticism directed towards the 1963 Corvette). A fibreglass sealer was then applied to ensure a good adherence of the two primer coats both of which were baked at a temperature between 250° and 275°F and then hand sanded. By the time the "Magic-Mirror" acrylic lacquer had been applied, a total of approximately four gallons of sealer, primer and lacquer had been used on each Corvette body!

After the body and chassis had been joined the final assembly procedures, which included installation of headlights, instrument panel, instruments, interior trim, carpet and seats, were completed.

Production of the new Corvette on the full-fledged St. Louis assembly line began in September 1962 and when subscribers to such car buff publications as *Road & Track* and *Car & Driver* received their November 1962 issues, the cover feature stories, to no one's surprise, dealt with the 1963 Corvette Sting Ray. From the first public display of the Sting Ray, Chevrolet minced no words about how it perceived its latest two-seater. *Corvette News* (Volume 5, Number 6, 1962) carried a quote from a Chevrolet styling spokesman that said, in part: "The word 'American' keynoted all of our preliminary discussions. The new Corvette was to be a broad-shouldered masculine American sports car." The very first Sting Ray ad, a lavish three-page colour affair which opened with two Corvettes (a coupe and convertible) passing each other on what appeared to be an endless ocean of lined macadam, proclaimed, "Only A Man With A Heart Of Stone Could Withstand Temptation Like This!" Although no publications chose to comment upon the Corvette's virtues as a seducer of the male sex, there was, at least in the American press, considerable praise for both its engineering and styling. *Sports Car Graphic* (November 1962) regarding it as "sleek and sexy" added "The Corvette really comes of age as a luxury, high-performance sports car". *Car Life* (December 1962) observed, "Tricky, twisting roads are this Corvette's meat" and without a great deal of difficulty concluded, "... this is the best Corvette yet!".

Though Zora Arkus-Duntov would have been happier if the production Sting Ray had weighed a bit less, he nonetheless was pleased with its final form. "For the first time", he remarked *(Corvette! America's Star-Spangled Sports Car,* by Karl Ludvigsen), "I now have a Corvette I can be proud to drive in Europe."

Perhaps the high point of public acclaim for the new Corvette came from *Car Life* magazine which gave the 1963 Sting Ray its "1963 Award for Engineering Excellence". "The Corvette", said *Car Life* (April 1963) "purely and simply has the best suspension and chassis mass-produced in the United States today." *Car Life* not only found the Sting Ray, when compared with previous Corvettes, "improved in almost every imaginable respect," but regarded it as a "fine showpiece for the American automobile industry, especially since it is produced at a substantially lower price than any foreign sports car or GT car of comparable performance."

The only real issues concerning the Corvette's new format involved the split rear window which seemed to arouse very strong negative feelings, the degree to which General Motors insisted upon adding extraneous bits and pieces of trim and simulated vents and grilles upon the Corvette's exterior, and the indifferent quality of its construction. The sports car market didn't regard these as obstacles to the Corvette's popularity. Output rose dramatically to 21,513 units which easily eclipsed 1962 (when 14,531 Corvettes were assembled) as the high point of Corvette production.

Prior to 1963 the Corvette had been the dominant production sports car in SCCA (Sports Car Club of America) competition. Its record included National Championships in three classes (Class B: 1957-1962, Class A: 1962, Class C: 1956) and numerous divisional titles. However, at virtually the same time the new Corvette was introduced, Carroll Shelby's Ford-powered Cobra debuted and its racing superiority over the Corvette (due in large part to its road weight of just over 2,000 pounds) soon became apparent. While not deprecating the Cobra's potent performance it's worth noting that total Cobra production in all forms from 1963-67 was only 1,011 cars whereas nearly 118,000 Corvettes were assembled over the same time span. In addition the Corvette's superiority in terms of ride, weather protection and overall accommodation needs to be factored into any equation attempting to deal objectively with the relative merits of what were really two rather different sports cars.

Chevrolet did, of course, amply demonstrate that it could create a Corvette able to deal effectively with the Cobra or for that matter the Ferrari GTO. This took the form of the Grand Sport Corvette of which only five were constructed. Alas, this project met a fate not unlike that of the SS Corvette. In 1963 GM President Roche once again affirmed the corporation's intent to adhere to the old AMA ban on participation in racing events. Chevrolet's general manager Bunky Knudsen had no recourse but to comply. However, before Chevrolet capitulated the Grand Sports travelled to the 1963 Nassau Speed Weeks where they convincingly outraced the Cobras and Ferrari GTOs.

The derailing of the Grand Sport's racing career barely touched upon the Corvette's popularity. Indeed, as measured by the 1964 model year output, which advanced to 22,229, it had no effect whatsoever!

The general appearance of the 1964 Corvette did not differ greatly from 1963 but without exception the changes made were for the better. Coupe models had a one-piece back window whose installation procedure eliminated the need for a rubber weather-strip. Common to both models was a restyled fuel filler cap with a smaller set of crossed flags mounted within a series of concentric circles. The superfluous simulated grille panels were removed from each side of the hood and the ribbed rocker panel beneath the doors now had fewer creases separated by black insert lines. The standard wheel covers had a simpler "Apple Pie" design. Coupe models were equipped with an internal ventilation system utilizing the air exhaust ports on the rear quarter panel (those on the passenger's side continued to be simulated). Significant changes were made to upgrade the comfort level of the Corvette's interior. Greater use was made of sound-proofing insulation blankets and the coupes now had six instead of eight body mounts of new rubber biscuit-type. Open models retained the original eight mounts, the four centre locations being fitted with the new type rubber mounts. Rounding out the major engineering changes for 1964 were variable rate front and rear springs that removed much of the harshness from the Corvette's ride.

1965 saw the Corvette

receive 4-wheel fixed caliper disc brakes and larger 7.75 x 15 in place of 6.70 x 15 tyres. Historically, 1965 was notable for being the only year a Corvette could be equipped with both fuel-injection and disc brakes. The Corvette continued to evolve into a more visually appealing automobile by virtue of the elimination of the twin depressions on the hood and the replacement of the dual, simulated exhaust ports on the front fenders with three functional louvres. The body sill was now a simple affair with a black centre line and a grille with vertical as well as horizontal bars helped identify the 1965 version as the latest Corvette.

If all had gone according to plan, 1966 would have been the last year for the original Sting Ray design. A new model whose styling was based upon the Mako Shark II show car of 1965 was slated to be its replacement in the 1967 model year. However, problems with front-end lift, and a profile that adversely affected front and rear vision pushed its introduction back a year. Appearance changes for 1966 were minor; a restyled lower body sill, standard pseudo-mag wheel covers and the inclusion of back up lights as part of the Corvette's basic lighting system were the most apparent changes.

The 1967 Sting Ray ended the short five year tenure of its basic body with class. Styling changes were again minor; new 6 inch slotted wheels and five instead of three, fender louvres. Unlike so many other American automobiles whose basic form under the influence of notorious "face lifting", suffered an annual deterioration, the Sting Ray's styling had steadily improved from its 1963 introduction. Moreover, its performance by virtue of the availability both of the legendary MKII-derived 396 and 427 cubic inch V8s had assumed a level formerly reserved for only a few of the world's most expensive sports cars. Indeed there were few solid reasons for the demise of the first generation Sting Ray. It remained an American automobile without

peer and as a grand touring automobile it was one of the world's greatest performance bargains. Thus it was obedience to a then fashionable styling cycle rather than obsolescence that brought the last of the Sting Rays built from 1963-67 down the St. Louis assembly line in July 1967.

H. 12355

EVOLUTION

1963 Model

1963 was the first year Corvettes were fitted with a trim data plate. Positioned on a cross bar beneath the glove compartment, it provided information concerning body style, interior trim, body number, paint number plus a date-built code. A smaller tag to the right of the trim data plate was stamped with the car's serial number, model year, type (coupe or roadster), plant of manufacture and upon occasion, dealer delivery date.

Two sets of identification numbers were stamped on a pad located at the right front side of the engine. The first was the engine serial number whose first digit represented the type of engine. Its final six digits corresponded to those of the car's serial number. A larger set provided information about the engine manufacturing site, date of manufacture and specific engine form.

The car's serial number was also found on the left side of the frame near the rear door pillar. It was also stamped on a flange of the manual transmission installed in 1964-67 Corvettes.

1963 model numbers were 837 for the Sport Coupe and 867 for the Convertible Coupe. Both models were identified as Sting Rays. Serial numbers for the 1963 model year ran from 100001 to 121513. A number of options – air-conditioning, power brakes, power steering, and leather seats were available for the first time on a Corvette.

Although the Sting Ray was virtually an all-new automobile some components were carried over from 1962. But many of these were modified for the new model. The three-speed manual transmission had a redesigned clutch gear bearing retainer, main-shaft extension and second and third shift levers. The four-speed manual gearbox had similar changes. The 12-volt electrical system was continued from 1962, but the D.C. charging system was replaced by a Delcotron A.C. system.

The fuel-injection system had a totally new external appearance and a number of important internal revisions. The intake manifold was still constructed of aluminium but it was now a two-piece unit without the internal bulk heads formerly used. A warm air choke system was added, a horizontal throttle shaft replaced the vertical shaft used previously and a larger diameter injector nozzle orifice was used.

When the Corvette was introduced in November 1962 a Z06 racing option priced at $1818.24 was offered for the coupe model, with the following components:

360hp, fuel-injection engine.
Four-speed all-synchromesh gearbox.
Positraction rear axle.
Kelsey-Hayes vacuum power brakes with dual circuit master cylinder.
Heavy-duty, finned brake drums with built-in cooling fans.
Heavy-duty metallic brake linings with multiple segment shoes.
Removable front brake scoops.
Vented brake flange plates.
Heavy-duty front and rear springs, shocks and front stabilizer bar.
Fibreglass, 36.5 gallon fuel tank.
Five case aluminium knock-off wheels.

Initially some Z06 Corvettes were delivered without the aluminium wheels (which were available separately as Regular Production Option RPO P48) and in early November 1962 a revamped brake drum with five cooling holes cut into its face was available to accept steel wheels in lieu of the aluminium versions. Early in 1963 (no later than March) the aluminium wheels were deleted from the Z06 package. Although the 36.5 gallon tank was listed in the original 206 lineup, in practice it never was a mandatory purchase. This change was made in order to allow Corvette convertibles to be purchased with the Z06 option which after deletion of the wheels and extra-capacity fuel tank listed for $1,295.

Major Production Changes. 1963 was the first year Four Season air-conditioning was available for the Corvette. Listed as a $421.80 (RPO C60) option on Sting Rays with the 250 and 300hp engine, it was not available until very late in the 1963 production run and only 278 cars were so equipped.

Beginning with serial number 101893 (approximately late December 1962) a redesigned parking brake lever was installed.

Corvettes built after November 30, 1962 had added interior heat insulation via the installation of a foil-coated fibreglass transmission tunnel cover.

Beginning on February 4, 1963 the 250hp and 300hp engine had a new primary ignition resistor installed to eliminate distributor point burning in cold-weather operation.

In late May 1963 the original oil pressure gauge with a 60 pound maximum reading was replaced by one with an 80 pound maximum reading.

Beginning with late June production a new gas filler cap and door with a spring catch in place of the older split-hinge version was installed.

1964 Model

The 1964 model year ran from September 1963 through July 1964 with serial numbers beginning with 100001 and ending with 122229. Two standard wheel cover designs were used during 1964. The early version, No. 3843389, had a small Argent silver outer concave band with the remaining, inner area in unpainted polished stainless steel. Sometime in November 1963, when approximately nine thousand 1964 model Corvettes had been assembled, a change was made to a wheel cover with the inner surface painted silver.

Starting in January 1964 Corvette bodies came from two sources, the original St. Louis Chevrolet facility and the A. O. Smith plant at Ionia, Michigan. Beginning with Serial Number 109678, bodies from St. Louis had an "S" preceding their body number. Those from A. O. Smith had an "A" prefix.

During December 1963 a new option, RPO K66, a full transistor ignition system priced at $75.35 became available for the L76, 365hp V8 and L84, 375hp, fuel-injected V-8.

1965 Model

1965 was the first year the Corvette, as well as all Chevrolet products, had a metal "Protect-O-Plate" attached to the last page of the owner's protection booklet. Corvettes continued to have vehicle identification plates attached to the crossmember beneath the glovebox door. The "Protect-O-Plate" provided information about the

Corvette's transmission, rear axle, exterior colour, interior trim, month of production, vehicle identification number, carburettor, engine identification and the name and address of the original buyer.

During March 1965 Chevrolet made several additions and revisions in the Corvette's optional equipment list. The most important development was the introduction of the L78, 425hp, Turbo-Jet 396 V8. In addition gold striped 7.75 x 15 – 4 ply nylon tyres (RPO T01) became a factory installed option. Power steering which previously had been available only with Corvettes powered by the 250 and 300 horsepower engines could now be ordered with Corvettes equipped with the RPO L79, 350hp V8. At the same time a side-mounted exhaust system with chambered pipes in place of regular mufflers became available for all 1965 Corvettes.

1966 Model

When the 1966 model year began the L36, and L72 427cid V8 engines were rated at 400 and 450 horsepower respectively. However, these ratings were apparently a bit too realistic for the conservative automobile insurance industry. As a result, Chevrolet retreated to less intimidating 390 and 425hp claims. Chevrolet did not offer

Powerglide with either of the Corvette's 427cid engines when the model began. Although it became an option for the 390hp version during March 1966. Another first for the Corvette during 1966 was the availability of head rests and the offering of the K19 "Air Injection Reactor", anti pollution option. Neither of these was commonly found on 1966 Corvettes. Only 9% were equipped with K19 and a mere 4% had the factory-installed head rests.

1967 Model

Nineteen sixty-seven was the first year an order copy attached to the gas tank was found on the Corvette. This valuable bit of Corvette paper provided the following information: identification number, trim options by name and number, date order received, expected date of production, order number, zone number, dealer number, model number and name, and paint name and number. Both the competition intended L88 engine and the L89 aluminium cylinder heads entered production in February 1967. The final 1967 Corvette, a convertible, with serial number 122940, left the St. Louis assembly line in July 1967.

H. 12355

Major Regular Production Options (RPO) 1963

No/Option		Price
L75:	300hp engine	$53.80
L76:	340hp engine	$107.60
L84:	360hp engine	$430.40
M20:	4-speed transmission	$188.30
M35:	Powerglide	$199.10
J50:	Power brakes	$43.05
N40:	Power steering	$75.35
J65:	Sintered brake linings	$37.70
G81:	Positraction differential 3.08:1 rear axle (250 and 300hp engines only)	$2.20
P48:	Cast aluminium wheels	$322.80

No	Option	Price
P92:	White sidewall, 6.70 x 15, 4 ply tyres	$31.55
941:	Sebring Silver paint	$80.70
T48:	Backup lights	$10.80
N34:	Woodgrained plastic rim steering wheel	$16.15
A01:	Soft ray tinted windows	$16.15
A02:	Soft ray tinted windshield only	$10.80
P91:	Blackwall nylon, 6.70 x 15, 4 ply tyres	$15.70
C07:	Removable hardtop	$236.75
898:	Saddle leather seat trim	$80.70
U65:	Signal-Seeking Radio	$59.20
C48:	Heater and defroster deletion	$137.75 (credit)
NO3:	36 gallon gas tank (coupe only)	$202.30

Major Regular Production Options (RPO) 1964

No/Option		Price
L75:	300hp engine	$53.80
L76:	340hp engine	$107.60
L84:	375hp engine	$538.00
M20:	4 speed transmission	$188.30
M35:	Powerglide	$199.10
J50:	Power brakes	$43.05
N40:	Power steering (250hp and 300hp engines only)	$86.10
J65:	Sintered brake linings	$53.80
681:	Positraction differential	$43.05
P48:	Cast aluminium wheels	$322.80
P92:	Whitewall tyres, 6.70 x 15, 4 ply tyres	$31.85
C07:	Removable hardtop	$236.75
U69:	AM-FM radio	$176.50
C48:	Heater and defroster deletion	$100.00 (credit)
NO3:L	36 gallon gas tank (coupe only)	$202.30

Major Regular Production Options (RPO) 1965

No/Option		Price
L75:	300hp engine	$53.80
L79:	350hp engine	$107.60
L76:	365hp engine	$129.15
L84:	425hp engine	$292.70
M20:	4 speed transmission	$188.30
M35:	Powerglide	$199.10
J50:	Power brakes	$43.50
N40:	Power steering (250hp and 300hp engines only)	$96.85
G81:	Positraction differential	$43.05
G91:	3.08:1 rear axle (250hp and 300hp engines only)	$2.20

No	Option	Price
P48:	Cast aluminum wheels	$322.80
P92:	Whitewall tyres, 7.75 x 15, 4 ply	$31.85
T01:	Goldwall tyres, 7.75 x 15, 4 ply nylon	$50.05
C07:	Removable hardtop	$236.75
Z01:	Comfort/Convenience Equipment	$16.15
U69:	AM-FM radio with power antenna	$203.40
C48:	Heater and defroster deletion	$100.00 (credit)
N32:	Teakwood rim steering wheel	$48.45
NO3:	36 gallon fuel tank (coupe only)	$202.30

Major Regular Production Options (RPO) 1966

No/Option		Price
L79:	350hp engine	$105.35
L36:	390hp engine	$181.20
L72:	425hp engine	$312.85
M20:	4-speed transmission	$184.30
M21:	4-speed, close ratio transmission	$184.30
M22:	4-speed, heavy duty transmission	$237.00
M35:	Powerglide automatic transmission	$194.85
J50:	Power brakes	$42.15
N40:	Power steering	$94.80
G81:	Positraction rear axle	$42.15
P48:	Cast aluminium wheels	$326.00
A01:	Soft ray tinted windows	$15.80
A02:	Soft ray tinted windshield only	$10.55
P92:	Whitewall tyres 7.75 x 14, 4 ply	$31.30
T01:	Goldwall tyres, 7.75 x 15, 4 ply, nylon	$46.55
C07:	Removable hardtop	$231.75
U69:	AM-FM radio, pushbutton	$199.10
C48:	Heater and defroster deletion	$97.85 (credit)
NO3:	36 gallon gas tank (coupe only)	$198.05
K66:	Full transistor ignition	$73.75

No	Option	Price
F41:	Special suspension (L72 only)	$36.90

Major Regular Production Options (RPO) 1967

No/Option		Price
L36:	390hp engine	$200.15
L79:	350hp engine	$105.35
L68:	400 hp engine	$305.50
L71:	435hp engine	$437.10
L88:	"Off Road" engine	$947.90
L89:	Aluminium cylinder heads for L71	$368.65
M20:	4-speed transmission	$184.35
M21:	4-speed, close-ratio transmission	$184.35
M22:	4-speed, heavy-duty transmission	$237.00
M35:	Powerglide automatic transmission	$194.85
J50:	Power brakes	$42.15
J56:	Heavy-duty brakes	$342.30
N40:	Power steering	$94.80
G81:	Positraction rear axle	$42.15
N14:	Side mounted dual exhaust	$131.65
N89:	Aluminium wheels 15 x 6L	$263.30
P92:	Whitewall tyres 7.75 x 15	$31.35
QB1:	Red stripe tyres 7.75 x 15	$46.65
U15:	Speed warning indicator	$10.55
U69:	AM-FM push button radio	$172.75
C48:	Heater and defroster deletion	$97.85 (credit)
NO3:	36 gallon gas tank (coupe only)	$198.05

H. 12355

SPECIFICATION

1963 Chevrolet Corvette

Model designation
Sport coupe – Model 837
Convertible coupe – Model 867
Built – St. Louis, Missouri September 1962 – August 1963

Serial Number range
100001–121513

Total production
21,513 (coupe – 10,594, convertible – 10,919)

Drive configuration
Front engine, rear-wheel drive

Engine

	Base	RPOL75	RPOL76	RPOL84
Bore x Stroke:	4 x 3.25in	4 x 3.25in	4 x 3.25in	4 x 3.25in
Displacement:	327cu.in	327cu.in	327cu.in	327cu.in
Maximum Power (bhp):	250 @ 4400rpm	300 @ 5000rpm	340 @ 6000rpm	360 @ 6000rpm
Maximum Torque (ft lb):	350 @ 2000rpm	360 @ 3200rpm	344 @ 4000rpm	352 @ 4000rpm
Carburetion:	Carter WCFB 4-barrel	Carter AFB 4-barrel	Carter AFB 4-barrel	Rochester fuel-injection
Compression Ratio:	10.5:1	10.5:1	11.25:1	11.25:1

Transmission
Optional:
Manual three-speed, (2.46, 1.53, 1.0), synchromesh on second and third. All synchromesh 4-speed (2.54, 1.89, 1.51, 1.0), available for base and L75, L76 and L84 engines. Standard axle ratio 3.36, optional 3.08. Powerglide 2-speed automatic, 3.36 axle ratio, available for base and L75 engines only. All synchromesh 4-speed (2.20, 1.64, 1.31, 1.0), available for L76 and L84 engines only. Standard axle ratio 3.70, optional 3.08, 3.36, 3.55, 3.70, 4.11, 4.56.

Rear axle
Hypoid, semi-floating.

Steering
Trailing relay type linkage, 20.2:1; available 17.6:1 (not offered with Powerglide).

Brakes
Hydraulic, self-adjusting. Drum dimensions: front 11 x 2.74in, rear 11 x 2.0in.
Total swept area 328sq. in.
Effective lining area 134.9sq. in.

Wheels	Pressed steel, bolt-on 15in diameter 5.5K. Standard tyre 6.70 x 15, 4 ply rayon blackwall, tubeless. Optional: Rayon whitewall, nylon blackwall. Suppliers: US Royal, BF Goodrich, Firestone, Goodyear, General.
Suspension (Front)	Independent, coil springs, short-long arms tubular shock absorbers, stabilizer bar spherical joints.
Suspension (Rear)	Independent, transverse, 9 leaf spring, three link, wheel driveshaft, camber control strut rod, trailing wheel spindle support arm.
Chassis	Perimeter unit with box section side rails and five crossmembers.
Bodywork	General Motors' designed, fibreglass with steel inner structure, assembled in St. Louis, Missouri of parts supplied by outside suppliers (Molded Fibreglass Products, Ashtabula, Ohio).
Weight	Convertible: 3,036 pounds. Coupe: 3,053 pounds.
Electrical system	Delco, 12 volt, Delcotron A.C. system positive earth Guide Lamp Division T-3 Safety headlamps.
Performance	(Model 837, 360hp engine 4-speed transmission, 3.7:1 rear axle) — 0-60mph, 5.6 sec. Standing start $\frac{1}{4}$ mile, 14.1 sec./102mph. Maximum speed, 151mph.
Fuel consumption	Since Corvettes were equipped with a multitude of engine-transmission combinations and were driven in a variety of fashions, a precise fuel consumption figure would be misleading. It is not difficult to have miles per gallon fall into the single digits if the Corvette is driven aggressively. On the other hand many contemporary owners report their cars can deliver nearly 20mpg at constant legal speeds (55mph) in the United States.

1964 Chevrolet Corvette

Model Designation	Sport Coupe-Model 837 Convertible Coupe-Model 867. Built — St. Louis, Missouri, September 1963 – July 1964.
Serial Number Range	100001-122229
Total Production	22,229 (Coupe 8304, Convertible 13,925).
Drive Configuration	Front engine, rear drive.

Engines	Base	L75	L76	L84
Bore & Stroke:	4 x 3.25in	4 x 3.25in	4 x 3.25in	4 x 3.25in
Displacement:	327cu.in	327cu.in	327cu.in	327cu.in
Maximum Power (bhp):	250 @ 4400rpm	300 @ 5000rpm	365 @ 6200rpm	375 @ 6200rpm
Maximum Torque (ft lb):	350 @ 2800rpm	360 @ 3200rpm	350 @ 4000rpm	350 @ 4600rpm
Carburetion:	Carter WCFB 4-barrel	Carter AFB 4-barrel	Holley 4150C 4-barrel	Rochester fuel-injection
Compression Ratio:	10.5:1	10.5:1	11.0:1	11.0:1

Transmission	Same as 1963, except for 4-speed available for Base and L75 engines which now had a 2.56 low gear.

Rear Axle	Same as 1963.
Steering	Same as 1963.
Brakes	Same as 1963.
Wheels	Pressed steel, bolt-on, 15 in. diameter 5.5K. Standard tyre – 6.70 x 15, two-ply-four-ply rated rayon blackwall. Optional: Rayon whitewall, nylon blackwall.
Suspension	Same as 1963.
Chassis	Same as 1963.
Bodywork	Same as 1963, except bodies were also assembled by the A. O. Smith Corp. Ionia, Michigan.
Curb weight	Convertible 3063lb/ Coupe 3053lb
Electrical system	Same as 1963.
Performance	(Model 837, 375hp engine, 4-speed, 4.11:1 rear axle) – 0-60, 5.6 seconds. Standing start $\frac{1}{4}$ mile, 14.2sec/100mph. Maximum speed, 134mph.

1965 Chevrolet Corvette

Model Designations:	Sport Coupe – Model 19437. Convertible Coupe – Model 19467. Built in St. Louis, Missouri, August 1964 – August 1965.
Serial Number Range	100001-123564*.
Total Production	23,562 (coupe 8,186, convertible 15,376) *The Corvette Restorer* (Volume 5, Number 4) notes a discrepancy exists between Chevrolet's production total and the production output as determined by serial number usage.
Drive Configuration	Front engine, rear drive.

Engines	Base	L75	L79	L76	L84	L78
Bore & Stroke:	4 x 3.25in	4 x 3.25in	4 x 3.25in	4 x 3.25in	4 x 3.25in	4.06 x 3.76in
Displacement:	327cu.in	327cu.in	327cu.in	327cu.in	327cu.in	396cu.in
Maximum power (bhp):	250 @ 4400rpm	300 @ 5000rpm	350 @ 5800rpm	365 @ 6200rpm	375 @ 6200rpm	425 @ 6400rpm
Maximum Torque (ft lb):	350 @ 2800rpm	360 @ 3200rpm	360 @ 3600rpm	350 @ 4000rpm	350 @ 4400rpm	415 @ 4000rpm
Carburetion:	Carter WCFB 4-barrel	Carter AFB 4-barrel	Holley R2818A 4-barrel	Holley R2818A 4-barrel	Rochester fuel-injection	Holley R3124A 4-barrel
Compression Ratio:	10.5:1	10.5:1	11.0:1	11.0:1	11.0:1	11.0:1

Transmission	Unchanged. The L78 and L79 engine available only with 2.20:1 low gear 4-speed transmission.
Rear axle	Same as 1963.
Steering	Same as 1963.
Brakes	Four wheel disc brakes, manufactured by General Motors' Delco-Moraine Division. Rotor dimensions: $11\frac{3}{4}$ x $\frac{1}{4}$ in. Total swept disc area — 461.2sq.in.
Wheels	Pressed steel, bolt-on, 15in. diameter 5.5K. Standard tyre 7.75 x 14, two-ply-four-ply rated rayon blackwall. Optional: Rayon whitewall, nylon Goldstripe (supplied by Goodyear or Firestone).
Suspension	Design unchanged from 1963 except front spring rates changed from 100lb/in to 80lb/in.
Chassis	Same as 1963.
Bodywork	Same as 1964.
Weight	Coupe (427cu.in/engine) — 3095lb. Convertible — 3063lb.
Electrical system	Same as 1963.

Performance	(Model 467, L75 engine 4-speed, 3.36:1, Positraction axle) -	(Model 467, L78 engine 4-speed, 4.70:1 Positraction axle) -
0-60mph:	7.5 sec.	5.7 sec
Standing start $\frac{1}{4}$ mile:	15.8sec/90mph.	14.1sec/103mph.
Maximum speed:	124mph.	136mph.

1966 Chevrolet Corvette

Model Designation	Sport Coupe — Model 19437. Convertible — Model 19467. Built in St. Louis, Missouri, September 1965–July 1966.
Serial Number Range	100001–127720.
Total Production	27,720 (Coupe — 9958, Convertible — 17,762)
Drive configuration	Front engine, rear drive

	Base	L79	L36	L72
Bore & Stroke:	4 x 3.25in	4 x 3.25in	4.25 x 3.76in	4.25 x 3.76in
Displacement:	327cu. in	327cu. in	427cu. in	427cu. in

Maximum Power (bhp):	300 @ 5000rpm	350 @ 5800rpm	390 @ 5400rpm	425 @ 5600rpm
Maximum Torque (ft lb):	360 @ 3200rpm	360 @ 3600rpm	465 @ 3600rpm	465 @ 4000rpm
Carburetion:	Holley 4-barrel R3367A (R3605A with K19 option)	Same as base	Holley 4-barrel R3370A. (R3606A with K19 option)	Holley 4-barrel R3247A
Compression Ratio:	10.5:1	11.0:1	10.25:1	11.0:1

Transmission	New standard 3-speed (2.54, 1.52, 1.0) all synchromesh transmission available only with base engine. 4-speed with 2.52 low available with all engines except L78. 4-speed with 2.20 low available with L79, L36, L72. Powerglide available only with base engine. New M22, heavy-duty 4-speed with 2.20:1 low available for L36 and L72.
Rear axle	Same as 1963.
Steering	Same as 1963.
Wheels	Same as 1965.
Suspension	Same as 1965.
Chassis	Same as 1963.
Bodywork	Same as 1964.
Weight	Coupe (327 cu. in engine) 3210lb. Convertible (427 cu. in. engine) 3270 lbs.
Electrical System	Same as 1963.
Performance (Independent road tests)	Model 19467 L72 engine, 3.36:1, Positraction axle) — 0-60mph, 5.4 sec. 0-100mph, 10.8 sec. Standing start $\frac{1}{4}$ mile, 112mph/12.8.sec. Top speed, 152mph.

1967 Chevrolet Corvette

Model Designation	Sport Coupe – Model 19437. Convertible Coupe – Model 19467. Built in St. Louis, Missouri., September 1966–July 1967.
Serial Number Range	100001–122940.
Total Production	22,940 (Coupe–8504, Convertible–14,436)
Drive Configuration	Front engine, rear drive.

Engines	Base	L79	L36	L68	L71	L88
Bore & Stroke:	4 x 3.25in	4 x 3.25in	4.25 x 3.76in	4.25 x 3.76in	4.25 x 3.76in	4.25 x 3.76in
Displacement:	327cu.in	327cu.in	427cu.in	427cu.in	427cu.in	427cu.in
Maximum Power (bhp):	300 @ 5000rpm	350 @ 5800rpm	390 @ 5400rpm	400 @ 5400rpm	435 @ 5800rpm	435 @ 5800rpm
Maximum Torque (ft lb):	360 @ 3400rpm	360 @ 3600rpm	460 @ 3600rpm	460 @ 3600rpm	460 @ 4000rpm	460 @ 4000rpm
Carburetion:	Holley 4-barrel, R3810A (R3814A with K19 option)		Holley 4-barrel R3811A (R3815A with K19 option)	*Triple Holley Primary R3660A 2-barrel Secondary R3659A		Holley 4-barrel R3418A
Compression Ratio:	10.25:1	11.0:1	10.25:1	10.25:1	11.0:1	12.0:1

*L68 with Powerglide: Primary R388A, Secondary R3659A.
L89 engine combines L71 engine with aluminium cylinder heads.

Transmission As 1966, Powerglide available with L36 and L68 engines.

Rear Axle Same as 1963.

Steering Same as 1963.

Brakes Same as 1965.

Wheels Pressed steel, ventilated, bolt-on, 15 in diameter, 6K.
Standard tyre 7.75 x 15 four-ply, rayon blackwall.
Optional – Rayon blackwall, nylon Redstripe (supplied by Goodyear, Firestone and U.S. Royal).

Suspension Same as 1965.

Chassis Same as 1963.

Bodywork Same as 1964.

Weight Same as 1966.

Electrical System Same as 1963.

Performance (Independent road tests) (Model 19437, 300hp, 4-speed, 3.36:1 axle) –
0-60mph, 7.8 sec.
0-100mph 23.1 sec.
Standing start $\frac{1}{4}$ mile, 16 sec/86.5mph.
Maximum speed, 121mph

ROAD TESTS

THE

CHEVROLET CORVETTE STING-RAY

AMERICAN sports cars in general are treated rather light-heartedly this side of the Atlantic, for, although their engines are well up in power output, with extraordinarily good torque figures, the U.S. market demands a very soft type of suspension and many creature comforts not in keeping with sports cars as we know them.

Not so the 1963 Corvette, which is a completely new car featuring a new body shape, new frame, and new type of suspension, and defies most of the established demands of the American market.

The wheelbase is now 98 ins., which is 4 ins. shorter than the 1962 car, and the weight distribution has now changed to 48 per cent. on the front and 52 per cent. on the rear. The body is still manufactured from glass fibre (double-skinned), and there are sub-frames of steel set in at the doors and under the cowl; the overall weight-saving is, however, only approximately 50 lb.

The front suspension is by double wishbones with coil springs and an anti-roll bar—in fact, it is as on earlier models. The rear suspension, though, is completely changed, being all-independent. The differential is chassis-mounted, and the rear wheels are located by trailing arms and torsion bars, suspension being afforded by a transverse leaf-spring; the open drive-shafts from the differential serve as a suspension link. Telescopic shock absorbers are mounted in front of the drive-shafts. The differential and the transverse leaf-spring are bolted to the chassis on rubber mounts, presumably to reduce noise. This layout reduces the unsprung weight to a minimum.

Steering is by a recirculating-ball system, and it is possible to change the ratio by simple steering-box adjustment from the standard of 19.6: 1 to 17.0: 1. This gives locks of 3.4 and 2.92 respectively. The steering wheel is also fully adjustable by a simple under-bonnet operation.

The chassis is lighter than before and has 12 mounting points for the body—these are steel reinforcements on the glass fibre. The torsional rigidity would appear to be adequate.

The brakes on our particular Sting-Ray were fitted with special metallic linings running in larger diameter drums affording 328.0 sq. ins. swept area, these being operated by a dual master cylinder and vacuum booster. These brakes have an interesting method of adjustment—the car automatically takes up the brakes when they are applied in reverse gear.

General Motors have used their well-tried and proved 5,340 c.c. V8 engine which produces 360 b.h.p. at 6,000 r.p.m. on an 11.25 compression ratio with Rochester fuel-injection. This power unit has enormously good torque (352 ft. lb.). A Delco alternator replaces the dynamo used on the 1962 cars, and a smaller flywheel allows the engine to be lower in the chassis. A freewheel fan is also fitted—this cuts out at speeds above 40 m.p.h.

The gearbox is the Borg-Warner four-speed with synchromesh on all gears with ratios of 8.14, 6.14, 4.85 and 3.27 to 1.

As with the specification, the appearance does not conform with established American practice either, and the car has extremely clean and purposeful lines with a minimum of chrome plate and fins. It does, however, have—rather unfortunately to my mind—false intakes on the bonnet and in the bodywork behind the front wheels. The front headlights are fitted with hoods which improve the aerodynamic line and no doubt increase the maximum speed, although we did not try to determine just what speed difference there was. The overall appearance of the car is extremely good and, judging by the comments received (especially from the fair sex!), the owner should not be disappointed.

The seating position is good, the seats themselves very comfortable, and the dashboard layout is one of the best I have seen. Immediately in front of the driver are both rev. counter and speedometer and these are flanked by fuel, oil pressure, water temperature and ammeter gauges. A pull-push switch controls the lights, which have a warning signal to tell the driver whether they are retracted or not. The headlight units are controlled separately by a switch underneath the dashboard. Above the propshaft tunnel is a clock and a radio, both items being standard

equipment. The heating and demisting switches are also to be found here. Two-speed windscreen wipers are fitted and these are extremely efficient.

The steering wheel, which is manufactured from aluminium, is dished and is fully adjustable for most drivers' requirements. This adjustment is controlled by a sliding-spline located between the bulkhead and the steering box itself. As explained earlier, the actual steering ratio can be altered.

The forward vision, very important with a car of this potential, is good and the wind-up windows, too, have the minimum of restricted vision. On our convertible test car the Perspex rear window was large and could not be criticized.

As was expected, the 360 b.h.p. engine was extremely flexible except below 1,000 r.p.m. The fuel-injection gave instant throttle response, and it was possible to accelerate away really hard from 30 m.p.h. in top. The engine revs extremely freely and the red line only starts at 6,300 r.p.m., which, believe it or not, the careless could easily exceed. Twin exhaust systems carried the gases to two tail pipes, these emitting the tell-tale note of a high-performance V8 engine. The alternator, which was mounted on the nearside front wing and belt-driven from the engine, would charge even when

the headlights, radio, flashers, etc., were all operating.

Mated to the engine by means of an extremely tolerant clutch running in an aluminium bellhousing was the Borg-Warner four-speed gearbox. Unlike most gearboxes fitted to high-performance cars in this country, it is extremely good with well-chosen ratios. Up and down changes could be made as fast as the hand could move and at no time did it answer back with that familiar grating noise. The clutch takes up instantly and smoothly, and these two units between them contribute largely to the enjoyment of driving this car. Reverse gear is engaged by lifting a slide on the gear lever and always worked smoothly and efficiently.

The rear axle copes admirably with the power and the independent rear end, and the positraction differential makes rapid take-offs simple manoeuvres.

The performance figures speak for themselves. The ¼ mile, the real tell-tale of any car's performance, was covered in 14 seconds dead. 30 m.p.h. came up in 2.2 secs., 50 in 4.1 secs., 60 in 5.4 secs. and 80 in 9.5 secs. The 100 figure was rather hackneyed by a stop-watch reading 14.2 seconds! It should be pointed out here that these figures were obtained

ACCELERATION GRAPH

SPEED AT 6000 R.P.M. IN TOP 135.1 M.P.H.

¼ MILE

CHEVROLET CORVETTE 'STING RAY'

M.P.H. / SECONDS

SPECIFICATION AND PERFORMANCE DATA

Car Tested: Chevrolet Corvette Sting-Ray two-door convertible, price £3,293, including P.T.
Engine: Eight-cylinders (two fours in V), 5,340 c.c. Push-rod operated overhead valves in light alloy heads. 360 b.h.p. at 6,000 r.p.m. Compression ratio 11.25 to 1. Rochester fuel injection with automatic choke. Coil and distributor ignition.
Transmission: Single dry plate clutch. Four-speed gearbox with all synchromesh. Ratios 8.14, 6.14, 4.85 and 3.70.
Chassis: Steel chassis with fibreglass body, independent four-wheel suspension by coil springs and double wishbones on the front with anti-roll bar, and transverse leaf spring, trailing arms and torsion bars on the rear. Drum brakes both front and rear, total brake area 328 sq. in. Twin master cylinders and vacuum booster. 670 x 15 tyres on bolt-on disc wheels.

Equipment: 12-volt lighting and starting. Rev. counter, speedometer, fuel gauge, petrol gauge, oil pressure gauge, ammeter, windscreen wipers and washers, heating, demisting, flashing direction indicators, radio, clock.
Dimensions: Wheelbase 8 ft. 2 ins. Track (front) 4 ft. 8½ ins., (rear) 4 ft. 7½ ins. Overall length 14 ft. 7 ins. Width 5 ft. 9½ ins. Weight (approx.) 30 cwts.
Performance: Maximum speed at 6,000 r.p.m. in top 137.1 m.p.h. Speeds in gears: 1st, 62 m.p.h., 2nd, 80 m.p.h., 3rd, 102 m.p.h., at 6,000 r.p.m. Standing quarter-mile 14 secs. Acceleration 0-30 m.p.h., 2.2 secs.; 0-50 m.p.h. 4.1 secs.; 0-60 m.p.h. 5.4 secs.; 0-80 m.p.h. 9.5 secs.; 0-100 m.p.h. 14.2 secs.
Fuel Consumption: 15 m.p.g.
Oil Consumption: approx. 1 pint per 100 miles.

predictability, and the limited slip differential played a good part in high speed motoring in these conditions.

We did not get an opportunity to try the car on the circuits as these were covered in snow during the period of test. We did establish, however, there was very little tendency to lift wheels when corners were taken really fast, and the front was remarkably stable.

It was rather unfortunate that John Bolster was unable to try the car because he rather likes big bangers, and I am sure he would have enjoyed this car as much as I did. Unluckily for him business kept him employed elsewhere and I must confess I did not complain too bitterly.

Finally my thanks must go to George Drummond, the owner of this delightful beast, who was kind enough to loan his personal transport on this occasion. George agrees wholeheartedly to what I say about the brakes and hopes that Dunlops will be able to provide some discs later this year. The tyres, too, although giving

using only 6,000 r.p.m. in the gears by special request of the owner.

In my opinion little advantage would have been gained by using the extra 500 r.p.m. available, as the power came in at 4,000 r.p.m. and gear changes dropped you back to approximately 4,500 r.p.m. The up changes were made at approximately 62, 80 and 102 m.p.h. which, to all intents and purposes, were for us the maximum speeds in the gears.

With such performance available one had one of the fastest cars on the road (if not the fastest—depends who's out that day). A criticism of American cars in general has always been that they are able to pass anything in a straight line with the exception of fuel stations, but this was not true of our car, which had a petrol consumption of 15 m.p.g. overall, which gave it a range of nearly 250 miles. On one occasion, however, the automatic choke stuck closed and we recorded a record figure, as far as I was concerned, of 6 m.p.g. before the trouble was rectified.

As a tester I have had the misfortune to drive cars with few brakes, but this car was the worst in this respect that I have ever experienced. With 328 inches of swept area with really hard metallic linings, one would have expected to find that together the servo and driver should have been able to retard the car's progress in an orderly fashion, but this was very rarely the case. The main trouble with the brakes was the fact that one could never rely on them and they tended to pull violently to the left at low speed—very off-putting for those in the slow lane!

I am afraid that drum brakes are just not adequate for a car which is likely to be driven consistently at speeds well over the "ton". General Motors must have difficulties in regard to their policy when it comes to fitting mechanical parts manufactured by other major concerns, but it would seem very short-sighted not to build disc brakes under licence until such time as they have fully developed their own.

The steering proved extremely good and was not unduly heavy in traffic, whilst straight line running at high speed was no problem. When the car was delivered for test the steering was adjusted for 3.4 turns from lock to lock and this necessitated a "handful of wheel" when negotiating the tighter roundabouts.

The suspension, although not soft, permitted the car to pitch under braking and roll under heavy cornering, in neither case

to an excessive degree, but sometimes a little off-putting if one was motoring on. Let me say here and now the handling was extremely good and seemed little affected by these slight tendencies. Fast open corners were this car's métier, and when the car was pushed beyond its limits it was still very ladylike in its behaviour. Slower corners, too, were negotiated at a fair rate of knots and no doubt could be taken faster with a more suitable steering ratio. The power could be used on all corners and traction was rarely lost through slight wheel spin or a jumping tail. In fact with the power on the tail sat really down on the road and gave the driver a great sense of security.

A criticism that could be made is the car does not lend itself to being driven slowly in traffic, and it is more difficult to make a gentle take off than it is to execute a full blooded racing getaway. The reason for this appears to be that the fuel injection provides no power below 1,000 revs., and it is necessary to let the clutch in at about 2,000 revs. minimum—the Kings Road tended to be rather nerve-racking in the rush hour.

In really wet conditions and snow the car proved extremely good by virtue of its

no trouble whatsoever, could be changed to advantage by fitting R5s. The tubeless tyres which are employed as standard equipment to my mind are not really suitable for speeds above 120 m.p.h. George has promised to let us time the car for maximum speed fitted with a high axle ratio and, he hopes, Dunlop discs and tyres. I shall look forward to this very much.

ROAD TEST 18/65

Seven liters can make a ton-and-a-half defy the laws of inertia!

MAYBE IT'S DIFFICULT TO FEEL SORRY FOR A CORPORATION THE SIZE OF GENERAL MOTORS, but they certainly deserve sympathy for the "Nervous Nellie" routine they've been forced into since withdrawing from racing. What was supposed to fill these pages was a track test of an optioned 427, a hundred of which are supposed to be built by January One and homologated with both FIA and SCCA. Since their retirement from active competition, Chevrolet has been beseiged by customers and dealers to at least make hardware available so they could go racing on their own. This program was strictly that; give the customer something to work

with. The package is still in the mill at this writing and MAY see a production line. If rumors are correct, it's nothing too wild; several alloy options — including cylinder heads — that enable you to reduce the curb weight to around 2600 pounds, and mild engine rework that puts output above 500 horsepower.

Anyhow, the optioned car didn't get here before our deadline so we settled for a "street" 427, figuring it wouldn't be very much different from a 396. Frank Milne, of Harry Mann Chevrolet — a local dealer enthusiastic about Corvettes — loaned us a brand-new unit with only 150 miles on the clock. Half-way down the block we noticed the difference and our staff photog

427 Sting Ray

was already complaining of whiplash. It's no secret that the Sting Ray is a heavy car, heavier than almost any sports car on the market. Even the 396 didn't take away the heavy "feel" of driving a Sting Ray, but the 427 does. Oh, brother, it does. We didn't even bother taking it to Riverside or Willow Springs for acceleration runs...all you need is a two-block-long straight. From a 70-mph cruising speed you can accelerate to the redline in top gear (140 mph) in roughly a mile. Sixty to 100 mph in top gear takes a mere 7.2 seconds. Tell us you'd like a hotter performing road machine than this and we'll call you some kinda nut!

Before the test, Milne asked us if we'd like a special set of tires on the car. Knowing it takes quite a tire to absorb that kind of horsepower, we quickly agreed. What he put on were Firestone Sports Car "200's"; 6.70's on the front and 7.10's on the rear in combination with the six-inch $330 optional alloy wheels. They were great; as good as most in sandy-surface or wet-surface conditions, and sticking like mad in the dry. The only noticeable drawback was a very high-pitched whine at high cruising speed. Yet this was relatively quiet and more than offset by an almost total absence of cornering squeal. Undoubtedly they had a considerable amount to do with the excellent roadability of the car. There was little wheel-spin from a standing start, excellent stopping stability under extreme braking, and cornering power in the One G Category. The 200's are available from Firestone, and Harry Mann sells them for $205 extra on an exchange basis, installed.

Unexpectedly, the 427 is not a strong understeerer when there's any bite to be had. It is *slightly* understeering going into a corner, and this changes to slight oversteer as soon as power is applied. The limit is reached with the rear end breaking loose all of a sudden and, even though it takes quick reflexes, a slight twitch of the wheel and an instant of lift with the accelerator foot will bring it back under control. But you have to be going gawdawful fast to reach the limit—very near competitive racing speeds.

The porcupine engine...which first saw the light of day as a 427, *not* a 396...is a beaut. There's gobs of low end torque and a willingness to grab revs that belies its size. It'll turn seven grand, so the 6500 redline is conservative. Making our top speed runs, we found it wanted to pull well past the redline and, with a 4.11 final-drive, 4000 rpm equaled 80 mph, making the speed of our test vehicle a very real 140 plus. With the optional close-ratio gearbox, you can grab a fabulous zero-60-mph time; it's first cog all the way. The four-speed, full-synchro box is the Muncie unit. It shifts firmly and positively, but has a little tendency to grunch in First and Reverse when it's hot. The center-pivot floats of the Holley carburetor completely eliminate any dumping or flat spots in the turns, but there is a definite hot-start problem, due apparently, to percolation. You have to hold the throttle on the floor and crank for a while to get it to fire up under these conditions.

While we're on the subject of temperature, it's interesting to note that, while our test car was not equipped with any power options, it ran a steady water temperature of 212F in an ambient of 75°F. This is worrisome—until you get in traffic with it and find it doesn't climb any higher. The cooling system is pressurized to 15 pounds, has a copper radiator, and—obviously—should have glycol instead of water at all times. As far as effect of the engine is concerned, modern V-8's with thin-wall castings operate fine at these temperatures. Heat in the cockpit is noticeable. The smooth-flowing cast-iron headers and twin exhaust systems that run beneath the chassis make excellent radiators that even the thick fiberglass can't insulate in warm weather. It would seem almost a must to have the whole system removed, sand-

Like the 396, the 427 is easily distinguished by the large and pointed hood bubble. As shown here, the powerful car really takes the corners.

Viewed from the rear, there's little different about the '66 Sting Ray except the ventilators missing from the quarter posts. Up front, however, is a very tasteful egg-crate grille replacing the previous design.

Top left shows the neat and very efficient instrumentation along with the simulated-wood steering wheel. At right, the wide, flat Firestones — in conjunction with the optional cast wheels — are ideal for this application, with only slight drawbacks in noise level. Behind them are huge disc brakes that really stop the heavy car from the high speeds it can reach. Below, the 427-inch Chevy takes up a lot of room, though there were no power options to contend with. Lower right, the new Holley carb, with center-pivot floats is the only fuel system available with the "porcupine" powerplants. Copper-core radiator is used with these engines.

blasted, and liberally coated with Sperex VHT paint.

Body changes to the 427 include the hood bubble that appeared with the 396 engine option, a very tasteful egg-crate grille, and the removal of the vents in the rear quarter of the roof. Not having an earlier 'Ray to compare it to, we suspect the seats have been raised, a bit, as we no longer had that "buried-below-the-dash" feeling we remembered in previous Corvette tests. Forward visibility is excellent, but we immediately missed the adjustable steering column option, as the wheel is a bit too close for personal tastes. Genuine carp department: that simulated-wood steering wheel is attractive and just the right size, but let your hands get the slightest bit damp, or greasy, and it becomes the slipperiest thing you've ever grabbed. As steering effort is fairly high—with no power option — driving gloves are a must.

With the optional suspension, the ride is *very* firm, pleasant enough for smooth roads, but almost uncomfortable on bumpy, wavey surfaces. Yet we logged almost 350 miles in one day of covering all kinds of roads, and neither driver nor passenger felt any overall discomfort. As a matter of fact, the firmness represented security as the right foot kept getting heavier and heavier.

Gas mileage is not the forte of the 427 Sting Ray. We found it easy to empty the 20-gallon tank of premium fuel; something in the neighborhood of 14 mpg. Conservatively driven, this figure would probably improve to 16 or 17 mpg, but we weren't in the mood for feather-footing with this kind of power and handling on tap. Incidentally, either the timing was slightly off or the 11-to-1 compression ratio is critical to detonation. It is advisable to use top-octane fuel, in the neighborhood of 105 Research. Our test car was equipped with transistorized ignition and, of course, the usual radio shielding required in a fiberglass car. There were no other spark problems. The $199.00 AM/FM radio worked beautifully. Lord, it ought to for that money! Seriously, it pulled in strong signals in areas we never believed it possible, with mountain ranges being no obstacle.

Other than the above, the new Sting Ray is pretty much like last year's. The bodywork gets better every year, and it's really first-quality this go-around. The base price of the 427 Ray is $4290; a pretty amazing figure for a high-performance limited-production machine. The options, like CR gearbox, engine goodies (that actually raise the output to 450 hp at something like 6200, but is underestimated to keep a couple of ambitious Eastern Senators from getting excited), tinted windshield, power windows, radio, etc., raise the list of this particular unit to $5400 delivered in Los Angeles. Add another six hundred odd bucks for the special tires and wheels — they're well worth the investment — and the total price is still under anything on the market that will match any of its individual attributes, let alone the sum of them. It's a really fine Grand Touring machine and the first Corvette we could get excited about owning!

— *Jerry Titus*

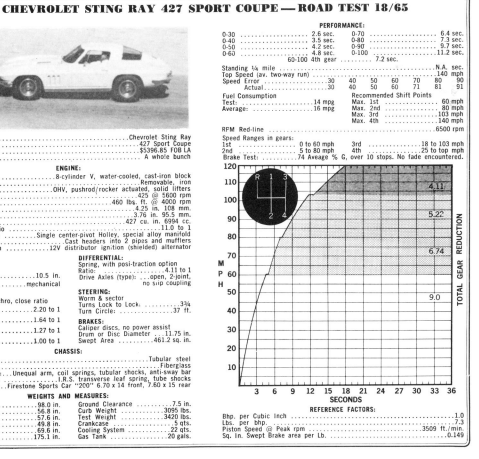

CHEVROLET STING RAY 427 SPORT COUPE — ROAD TEST 18/65

PERFORMANCE:

0-30	2.6 sec.	0-70	6.4 sec.
0-40	3.5 sec.	0-80	7.3 sec.
0-50	4.2 sec.	0-90	9.7 sec.
0-60	4.8 sec.	0-100	11.2 sec.
	60-100 4th gear	7.2 sec.	

Standing ¼ mile .... N.A. sec.
Top Speed (av. two-way run) .... 140 mph

Speed Error	.30	40	50	60	70	80	90
Actual	.30	40	50	60	71	81	91

Fuel Consumption
Test: .... 14 mpg
Average: .... 16 mpg

Recommended Shift Points
Max. 1st .... 60 mph
Max. 2nd .... 80 mph
Max. 3rd .... 103 mph
Max. 4th .... 140 mph

RPM Red-line .... 6500 rpm

Speed Ranges in gears:
1st .... 0 to 60 mph   3rd .... 18 to 103 mph
2nd .... 5 to 80 mph   4th .... 25 to top mph
Brake Test: .... .74 Aveage % G, over 10 stops. No fade encountered.

Vehicle .... Chevrolet Sting Ray
Model .... 427 Sport Coupe
Price (as tested) .... $5396.85 FOB LA
Options .... A whole bunch

ENGINE:
Type .... 8-cylinder V, water-cooled, cast-iron block
Head .... Removable, iron
Valves .... OHV, pushrod/rocker actuated, solid lifters
Max. bhp .... 425 @ 5600 rpm
Max. Torque .... 460 lbs. ft. @ 4000 rpm
Bore .... 4.25 in. 108 mm.
Stroke .... 3.76 in. 95.5 mm.
Displacement .... 427 cu. in. 6994 cc.
Compression Ratio .... 11.0 to 1
Induction System .... Single center-pivot Holley, special alloy manifold
Exhaust System .... Cast headers into 2 pipes and mufflers
Electrical System .... 12V distributor ignition (shielded) alternator

CLUTCH:
Single disc, dry
Diameter .... 10.5 in.
Actuation .... mechanical

TRANSMISSION:
4-speed, full-synchro, close ratio
Ratios: 1st .... 2.20 to 1
2nd .... 1.64 to 1
3rd .... 1.27 to 1
4th .... 1.00 to 1

DIFFERENTIAL:
Spring, with posi-traction option
Ratio: .... 4.11 to 1
Drive Axles (type): ... open, 2-joint, no slip coupling

STEERING:
Worm & sector
Turns Lock to Lock 3¾
Turn Circle: .... 37 ft.

BRAKES:
Caliper discs, no power assist
Drum or Disc Diameter ... 11.75 in.
Swept Area .... 461.2 sq. in.

CHASSIS:
Frame: .... Tubular steel
Body: .... Fiberglass
Front Suspension: ... Unequal arm, coil springs, tubular shocks, anti-sway bar
Rear Suspension: .... I.R.S. transverse leaf spring, tube shocks
Tire Size & Type: .. Firestone Sports Car "200" 6.70 x 14 front, 7.60 x 15 rear

WEIGHTS AND MEASURES:
Wheelbase: .... 98.0 in.
Front Track: .... 56.8 in.
Rear Track: .... 57.6 in.
Overall Height .... 49.8 in.
Overall Width .... 69.6 in.
Overall Length .... 175.1 in.

Ground Clearance .... 7.5 in.
Curb Weight .... 3095 lbs.
Test Weight .... 3420 lbs.
Crankcase .... 5 qts.
Cooling System .... 22 qts.
Gas Tank .... 20 gals.

REFERENCE FACTORS:
Bhp. per Cubic Inch 1.0
Lbs. per bhp. 7.3
Piston Speed @ Peak rpm .... 3509 ft./min.
Sq. In. Swept Brake area per Lb. 0.149

(chart: TOTAL GEAR REDUCTION — 4.11, 5.22, 6.74, 9.0 — vertical axis MPH, horizontal axis SECONDS)

OWNER'S VIEW

Bob Ackerson interviewed two owners of Corvettes and asked them identical questions. The first was W. L., the owner of a 1967 Corvette with the 435hp – 427 V-8. The second was T. S. who owns a very rare 1963 ZO6 Coupe.

RA – What first interested you in Corvettes?
WL – My interest dates back to 1967 when I was a helper on an S.C.C.A. racing team. I began to realize the 1967 had a lot of features I liked.
TS – I've liked Corvettes for years, but to me the '63 is the sleekest looking of the '63-'67 coupes with its rear window line. The ZO6 is especially appealing to me because they were bought and sold strictly for racing.

RA – When and where did you buy your car?
WL – I bought my car in May 1972 after spending eighteen months looking at twenty 1967 Coupes.
TS – I was looking for a '63 Coupe and when I purchased this car in April 1977 it appealed to me because it was an original fuel-injected car.

RA – What condition was your car in?
WL – Its condition was very sound. The owner was looking for someone who would take care of the car.
TS – The car basically looked like a street racer. But it was very intact in terms of key components. But since it was a street racer with the wrong wheels, tyres, shifter, etc., it had to be brought back from the dead.

RA – Were the problems your car had common to that year's model?
WL – The biggest drawback of the '67 is the 6 inch Rally wheels. You can't turn without the tyres hitting the wheel wells. But there aren't any particularly weak components. The rear wheel bearings are a problem in all '63-'67 Corvettes.
TS – I really didn't have any actual problems because in September 1977 I went into a total restoration of the car.

RA – What repairs and renovations were completed?
WL – I had to do several minor projects to return the car to a completely stock condition. The suspension had been jacked up, wider wheels had been mounted and a mechanical instead of vacuum operation of the carburetors had been installed.
TW – Every nut and bolt was removed. Nothing was left untouched.

RA – Would it have been more economical to have purchased a car in worse condition than yours was originally?
WL – I would not get into the restoration car, basket case or project car. It's an absolute waste of time. The cost is astronomical. To even find the parts is difficult because so many are no longer made.
TS – If my car had been in better condition when I bought it, it would have been out of my price range. If you buy a car in tough shape hopefully you can put that much more into the car. For example an interior that is reasonably good means nothing if you are going to put a new one in anyway.

RA – Have you experienced difficulty in obtaining any parts?
WL – Yes. There were several parts I had a good deal of problems getting. One that was a real challenge was the corner moulding on the windshield trim. I finally located a Chevrolet dealer in Maryland who had them. They originally sold for $7.00 and he was selling them for $35.00.
TS – Parts are tough to find. My solution was to buy as many Corvette publications as possible and constantly go through the ads. When you see a part that's priced right you have to jump right on it.

RA – What kind of performance and handling does your car have?
WL – I can honestly say for mass-produced cars, not counting any of the Ferraris and similar exotic cars, there were probably only two cars that were faster than the 435/427 Corvette; the L88 which was never intended to be used on the street anyway and the AC Cobra. But that was it. The 435/427 Corvette was a total brute when it came to performance. Nothing could perform like it. The handling, though, left a lot to be desired. It wasn't that terrific. You just couldn't get wide enough tyres for it. Compared to its peers, it was a great handler but I'm a highly critical driver and from that perspective it wasn't all that good.
TS – Fuel-injection is very responsive. You touch the gas and you have instantaneous response. The special brakes are kind of funny to drive when they're cold. You have to drive the car for five minutes to get them heated before they really begin to feel as if they are functioning properly. The original owner had the car up to 130mph in competition at Watkins Glen. But it still wasn't competitive with the Cobras.

RA – Is your car in regular, everyday use?
WL – When I first bought the car I drove it daily, except on rainy days, during the warm months. But I

never drove it in the snow. Since the car was new it has always been stored in the winter. After 1978 it became a weekend-sunny-day car. Parts were becoming harder to get, the value was becoming greater and so was my fear of people hitting or scratching it.

TS – The car is never driven on the road. Since it's trailered to and from shows, it's unlikely that it's driven more than two miles a year.

RA – How practical is the Corvette as an everyday car?

WL – When our children were small they were able to sit in the back. It didn't bother them. Today of course, I couldn't legally do that because I'd have to install restraining seats for them. We took a ten day trip with it in 1973 and parked it in motel parking lots and went to sleep and never gave a thought that it wouldn't be there in the morning.

TS – As far as an everyday car I don't think any Corvette qualifies. They all leak and even driving them on a limited basis you have to have a screwdriver and a pair of pliers with you all the time.

RA – Has your car won any prizes in concours or similar events?

WL – I've never personally felt it was a concours-type car and it's just earned some second and third place trophies at several small shows. Initially the shows were fun but Corvette shows in recent years have become so competitive that we've stopped going. It seemed as if there were too many people trying to find fault with your car. We never really showed the car in a serious vein.

TS – The primary show I was really tickled pink about was the Sixth Annual Corvette Revue sponsored by the Glen Regional Corvette Club. It is a very prestigious show. They had three judges on my car for about an hour, but it won both Best of Class and Best of Show. Every show (about seven) I went to in 1983 I came home with at least two trophies.

RA – What Corvette clubs do you belong to?

WL – Probably the best, most informative club I joined was the National Corvette Restorers Society. They believe in encouraging peope to drive their Corvettes and I think that's great.

TS – I belong to the National Corvette Owners' Association which is a very informative club with an excellent monthly newsletter. I'm also a member of both the National Corvette Restorers Society and the National Council of Corvette Clubs. All are valuable for information and parts. I never would have been able to purchase my original 36 gallon tank if I hadn't belonged to those clubs.

RA – Is there a Corvette specialist whom you found particularly useful?

WL – Long Island Corvette Supply has been a great source for many otherwise hard to find parts.

TS – Eugene Tibbils of Tibbils Auto Electric Service in Rochester NY was invaluable. He is a master mechanic-craftsman whose skill was a valuable asset to my restoration project.

RA – How would you sum up the enjoyment you get from your Corvette?

WL – I believe the honest answer to that question is that only people who have had the relationship with an automobile that I've had can understand the gratification a person gets from driving a car of that status. It's not the fact that it's

a Corvette. It's the fact that it is a well maintained, fast, exciting automobile that possesses all the things you could want in an automobile.

TS – It's great to talk to people that owned a '63 back when they were new. It's very satisfying to meet people who know what they are talking about.

RA – What advice would you give to potential owners of the 1963-67 Corvettes?

WL – If you want a car that's really going to be a fun car to own and very possibly appreciate in value, then I would get one of these three Corvettes: a 1963 coupe with fuel-injection, a 1965 (either model) also with fuel-injection or a 1967 (either model) with the 435 horsepower engine. Be sure of what you're getting. Some people have bought Corvettes with taxi cab or truck engines!

TS – Set your price range. Always check the frame carefully. Also check for originality of the body, engine and transmission. When you find a car that meets your expectations, buy it!

H.12355

BUYING

Next interviewed was Gary Enck of Otego, New York who, since purchasing his first Corvette in 1969, has owned (and sold) nearly 70 Corvettes. Known nationally and internationally as a purveyor of quality Corvettes he has clients worldwide.

RA – What do you regard as the strong and weak points of the 1963-67 Corvette?

GE – Any of the 1963-67 higher performance cars are going to require extra maintenance. For example, those Corvettes with solid lifters require more frequent valve adjustment. If you are purchasing one with fuel-injection you will have to learn a little bit about its operation. If you let it sit for a time with gas in the unit you can have problems. It's best to start it occasionally and run fresh gas through it. This prevents gasket shrinkage and the formation of shellac. The 1965, and up, models with the big blocks require a fair number of periodic adjustments to prevent the engine from going to hell if you get on it, which people sometimes do with these things. The 435hp/427 has three carburettors and you have to keep them and your fuel lines from leaking which often is a problem if the car isn't used frequently.

It's quite a different story with the low horsepower (250 and 300hp) small blocks and the 390-400hp 427s. My wife has one and we use regular gas in it and it never fails to perform properly. Compared to the other engines they're practically maintenance free.

The 1965-67 models have disc brakes and if the car sits for an extended period, there's a good chance moisture will get into the brake calipers and cause corrosion and leaks. Today they have stainless steel sleeved calipers and silicon fluid which prevents this from happening for a long time.

RA – How about comparing the Corvette to other sports cars. Does it have a measurable advantage in terms of durability and reliability?

GE – I would have to say the Corvette is a far smarter purchase. Since it is a Chevrolet a good percentage of its replacement parts are available at any Chevrolet dealership or supply house.

RA – How you do you feel about the 1963 Corvette? It has a reputation for inferior workmanship.

GE – When the '63s came out they were like the '68 and even the '84. It was a new design and they had problems with it. They had, for example, problems with the fibreglass in certain areas.

RA – What are some of the basics you look for in a 1963-67 Corvette you are considering for purchase?

GE – There are a few things that tell me immediately what type of care the car has had. If you open the door and it drops down half an inch and the upholstery is worn and tattered, then you know the car hasn't been well treated. Very few people who don't take care of the outside of the car, take good care of its mechanical workings. There isn't however, any one thing I think you can look for. I compare every Corvette to my original 1970 LT1 with 13,000 miles. That's my guide since I know what kind of care its had.

RA – Do Corvettes, because of their special status, tend to receive treatment that's different from that of the typical American car?

GE – Some people buy a 1963-67 Corvette and even today, when they are starting to be worth quite a bit of money get out their saw, cut the fenders [wings] and put flares on them! That may be alright if the car is in poor condition to begin with. But to take a car that's never been abused and do that is sacrilegious.

There are many people who really respect this car and there are others who would be better suited to drive an old pickup.

RA – Is there a point of no return for a 1963-67 Corvette where it is beyond saving?

GE – It depends on what the would-be owner wants when he's done. If you have a limited budget and lots of time you can do most anything. If they have a little more money and simply want a recreation-type project would recommend a car needing minor restoration.

Although the 1963-67 Corvettes are worth more and more each year, there is a point where the condition is so poor you might just forget about it. If the car is wrecked and the frame is rotted there's no value there other than parts value; better look for something different.

RA – Considering the areas of bodywork, interior and mechanical components – are there any areas where the 1963-67 Corvettes are particularly vulnerable to problems?

GE – The body is fibreglass of course, but you mentioned the frame. If a car has been driven where a great deal of salt is placed on the road in the winter months, the salt will eventually eat the frame. On the Corvette there is an area right behind the doors where the frame takes a 90° bend. That general area will rot and I usually check that region very carefully. The other plate is right along the rocker panel [sill] area. You should also raise the hood and look at the A-frame area, the brake lines and the metal fluid lines. If they are all scaly and what not, that's a telltale the car has been through a good deal of salt.

RA – How about the interior – any weak spots?

GE – The driver's seat will usually wear where you slide in and out. The seat piping will wear. It's important to note the seats are interchangeable. The door panels have a tendency to crack but they are reproducing items such as these. In fact, you can buy an entire interior for several hundred dollars so that's not really a problem.

RA – Are there any serious mechanical short falls or weak spots in the Corvette?

GE – There really aren't any major ones. The main thing is to determine if the car has the equipment that it should have. Nolan Adams is currently preparing Volume 2 of his *Corvette Restoration Guide* which will deal with the 1963-67 Corvettes. If that book is anywhere as informative as his first book it should be a must for anyone who wants to buy or restore a '63-'67 'Vette.

RA – How durable is the Corvette's rear suspension?

GE – They do have six universal joints in the rear end and they are bound to get some wear. The rear wheel bearings, because they are hard to lubricate and disassemble have a tendency to go, but you usually have some warning. It isn't something that happens overnight.

RA – Is there any one particular engine-transmission combination that you feel is most appropriate for the typical owner.

GE – If you want a 1963-67 Corvette for Sunday afternoon touring and a nice leisurely drive without any problems, I strongly recommend the hydraulic lifter, lower compression models. They would range from the 250-300hp 327s to the 390 and 400hp 427s. These latter engines will probably out-perform some of the higher performance small blocks and yet be as docile as the 250hp 327. I drove my first Corvette with the 300hp engine over 20,000 miles

and all I ever did was minor maintenance. You can get so much more enjoyment out of a car if you don't spend all of your weekends under the hood. That would be my recommendation.

RA – Let's look at this from another perspective: the person who is buying a Corvette and has an interest in its investment potential. Do we go in a different direction and look for a more powerful one?

GE – If he/she wants a 1963-67 Corvette only for investment and plans to drive it no more than a couple of hundred miles a year then there are several points to consider. Unrestored originality is the main key. The original car is the fairest of all. It doesn't have to be perfect. They had imperfections when they were new. After originality, look for options; the more the better. Then look for documentation such as the original window sticker, purchase invoice, original owner's title. An original car with documentation is worth a good, solid 25% more than the same car without the documentation.

You have to be careful of bogus cars since many people are making false engine stampings. If the car is authentic the numbers have to match. They had numbers on the engine, transmission, rear end, the frame, everything is numbered. So you can, with a little careful searching and research, determine the authenticity of any Corvette.

One of the most expensive Corvettes of the 1963-67 group, aside from the L88, is going to be the 1967 400hp, air-conditioned, car with options. They only made a few and even fewer with the four-

speed. The big blocks seem to be more collectable because of the desirability of most cars from that great performance era.

RA – What does your crystal ball have to say about future Corvette values?

GE – I thing the prices are going to continue to escalate. I've always felt that an original, unblemished, low-mileage car is worth as much, or more, than a new model and they have maintained this relationship throughout the years. The 1963-67 models are already headed in the upward direction. They're starting to appreciate tremendously and they've gained more value in the past 12 months than they have in a long time.

RA – Could you sum up your advice to the prospective owner of a 1963-67 Corvette?

GE – I'd like to underscore the importance of knowing who your seller is, learning something about the car and about the people who used to own it. Corvettes have a very high theft rate and you want to be sure the car you are buying has never been stolen. Don't be afraid to get the serial number of the car and call it in to the authorities. Before you spend that kind of money you ought to know the thing is right. Buy it with your head, not your heart ...

H. 12355

CLUBS, SPECIALISTS & BOOKS

The 1963-67 Corvette's outstanding performance, unique status among American automobiles and appealing styling are just three of many reasons why hundreds of active Corvette clubs are currently growing in membership and expanding their activities. Some clubs specialize in social events, while others lean towards either concours or competition events.

Clubs

For both the serious Corvette enthusiast or the beginner who wishes to become as familiar as possible with the Corvette, membership of the **National Corvette Restorers Society,** 6291 Day Rd, Cincinnati, OH, 45247, USA is a good choice. This organization, as its name implies, caters to the owner who wishes to restore his Corvette to original condition. The technical advisers of the NCRS whose speciality is the 1963-67 Corvette are precise, accurate and knowledgeable. Their expertise not only has been of great value to restorers but their close attention to detail has contributed to the correction of many historical errors that have found their way into Corvette literature. The NCRS quarterly publication *The Corvette Restorer Magazine* has exceptional editorial content and represents a treasure trove of Corvette information.

With well over 262 affiliated clubs and a membership in excess of 8000 the **National Council of Corvette Clubs,** P.O. Box 325, Troy, Ohio 45373-0325 USA, both publishes an excellent bi-monthly, *Blue Bars,* and provides the expertise for the sanctioning of numerous competition events. Its annual national convention is a week long extravaganza of concours shows, rallies, drag racing, low and high speed events plus socializing that leaves no Corvette owner in attendance disappointed.

In Europe, the **Swiss Corvette Club International,** Kurt G. Keischer, President, Zimmelstrasse 34a, CH-Unterageri (ZUG), holds an annual Vette-Euro-Meet on a European race course of renown which provides an abundance of social, competition and concours events.

In the UK the **Classic Corvette Club – UK,** 143 Smarts Green, Flanstead End, Chestnut, Herts, EN7 6BD, has over 110 members and publishes the quarterly, *News-Vette.*

Specialists

The Corvette is unique among sports cars in that it can be serviced at virtually any of the thousands of Chevrolet dealerships worldwide. But the popularity of the 1963-67 model has spawned a plethora of specialist firms. Among the more prominent are:

Corvette America, Box 427, Boalsburg, PA 16827 USA. (Corvette interior components).

Herb Adams Very Special Equipment USA, 100 Calle Del Oaks, Del Ray Oaks, CA 93940 USA. (Performance equipment).

Claremont Corvette, Chimney Mill, Claremont Road, Newcastle upon Tyne, England. (Chevrolet Corvette Specialists).

Corvette Specialties of Maryland, 3422 Pine Circle South, Westminster, MD 21157 USA. (Specializing in 1953-67 new, used and reproduction parts).

Long Island Corvette Supply, 62 Roosevelt Ave. Massapequa Park, NY 11762 USA. Phone – 516-541-9829. (Offers an extensive inventory of 1963-67 Corvette parts).

Walters Engineering, 7252 SW 55 Avenue, Miami, FL 33143 USA. (Specializing in fasteners and such small parts as nuts, bolts and grommets).

Books

Major volumes that contain relevant information relating to the history, restoration and maintenance of the 1963-67 Corvette include the following:

Corvette: A Piece of the Action by William Mitchell and Allan Girdler (published by Automobile Quarterly).

Vette Vues Fact Book of the 1963-67 Sting Ray by M.F. Dobbins (published by M. F. Dobbins).

Corvette: America's Star-Spangled Sports Car by Karl Ludvigsen (published by Automobile Quarterly).

The Best of the Corvette Restorer, 1953-67 (published by Michael Bruce Associates).

The Best Of Corvette News, edited by Karl Ludvigsen (published by Automobile Quarterly).

PHOTO GALLERY

1. The 1963-64 Corvettes used identical door panels. The door release knob on the 1963 is black. The following year it was chromed, matching the handle and window winder. The upper door reflector also functions as the door lock control.

2. Late in the 1963 model run Chevrolet replaced the older exposed hinge fuel filler door with this version.

3. The 1963 Sting Ray coupe's split rear window was originally an object of considerable debate and controversy.

4. The same circular antenna base was used for the 1963 and '64 Sting Ray. On subsequent models it was hexagonally shaped.

6

7

5. Four different upholstery patterns were used from 1963 to 1967. This format, with narrow pleats was found on the 1963 and '64 models. The seats of this 1963 ZO6 coupe are finished in leather which was a first-time option that year.

6 & 7. Two views of the 1963 Corvette's fuel-injection system.

8. The Corvettes of 1963 and '64 were fitted with crossed-flags insignia.

9. Two external mirror styles were used in 1963. Both had the Chevrolet bow tie logo but the second version used after approximately 12,300 Corvettes had been produced, had this smoother base and swivel head.

8

9

10

10. The 1963 Corvette's optional aluminium knock-off wheels. Some were also delivered with two instead of three knock-off ears.

11 & 12. An open and shut case, the Sting Ray's T-3 headlights.

13. This style of rear deck identification script was used from 1963 through 1965.

14. This type of exterior door handle with raised sections was used throughout the 1963 model year and part way through 1964.

11

12

13

14

15

17

16

18

15. The 1963 Corvette's simulated hood grille. Constructed of aluminium its background was flat black.

16. The interior of the 1963 coupe. The concave shape of the shifter boot was unique to the 1963, as were the solid inner circles of the instruments. A warning buzzer was activated when the rpm level reached 6500 on 360hp engined models.

17. This 1963, ZO6 coupe was in its early years an SCCA competitor. That helps to explain its lack of back-up lights. Corvettes with that feature had their inner rear lights replaced with reversing lamps.

18. This front fender emblem was used for 1963 and '64 Corvettes equipped with fuel injection.

19

20

19 & 20. The ultimate Corvette for 1963: the ZO6 Coupe!

21. The original Corvette prototype (EX-122), which was exhibited at the 1953 General Motors Motorama, as it appears today.

21

22. The 1963 coupe's controversial two-piece rear window was replaced by a single expanse of glass the following year.

23. Air-conditioned 1963 and 1964 Corvette coupes had this decal affixed to the right side of their rear window. Convertibles had the same decal located on the passenger side window. This coupe was one of just 1988 '64 Corvettes with air-conditioning.

24. The base 250hp, 327cid Corvette engine of 1964.

25. The instrument panel of the 1964 Corvette. Beginning that year the gauge covers were glass instead of plastic. The centre circles were black on the 1964 model. On models with the 250hp engine the tachometer is redlined at 5200rpm.

26. The 1964 glovebox door was of metal construction instead of fibreglass as used on the 1963 Sting Ray.

22

23

24

25

26

27

28

29

27. The centre console of a 1964 coupe equipped with air-conditioning, but without radio. This makes for a rare combination since 1988 Corvettes that year were ordered with air-conditioning but only 1295 were delivered without radios.

28. The 1964 coupe interior provided plenty of luggage space for serious grand touring. The carpeting was colour-keyed to the instrument panel.

29. As in 1963, the 1964 Corvette instrument panel positioned all major gauges within easy viewing distance of the driver. All 1964 models had 80lb oil pressure gauges.

30. The exhaust bezel on 1964 models was, in comparison to the unit used in 1963, of a larger diameter.

30

31. The Corvette's roof vents were reshaped for 1964. The set on the driver's side was functional. A switch on the dash controlled operation of a blower motor mounted in the rear body panel.

32. The Corvette's non-functional side fender vents were unchanged from 1963 to 1964. However the 1964 model has a new ribbed rocker panel with black inserts.

33. The 1963 and 1964 models shared the same grille design with thin horizontal bars.

34. Removal of the artificial hood grilles for 1964 was a step in the right direction. Small drain holes were found in the lower edge of the hood indentations.

35. The headlight housing of the 1964-67 Corvette was of steel construction. In 1963 it was plastic.

36. The Corvette's cowl-mounted interior air intake. The standard windshield washer jet can be seen adjacent to the wiper arm.

31

32

33

34

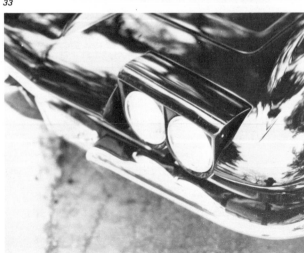

35

36

37. The 1964 Corvette's standard equipment wheel cover.

38. The Corvette's front end appearance was dramatically altered when the headlights rotated into their operating position.

39. All 1963-67 Corvette hoods were forward-hinged.

40. A competition-modified 1965 Corvette in action at Atlanta, Georgia.

37

38

39

40

41

42

41. A 1965 convertible in road-racing form.

42. Altered for drag-racing the 1965 Corvette assumes an ominous appearance.

43. Only 771 Corvettes were ordered with fuel-injection in 1965. The off-road exhaust system as fitted to this 1965 convertible was a mid-year option.

43

44

45

46

47

48

44. The fuel-injected engine for 1965 was rated at 375hp.

45. The wide-pleated seats were used only on the 1965 model.

46. The 1965 dash arrangement. The flat black gauge centres were common to all the 1965-67 models.

47. A 1965 convertible with the optional knock-off aluminium wheels.

48. Interior arrangement of the 1966 coupe. The glovebox door cover is brushed aluminium on all 1964-67 models.

49. The 1965 instruments do not have the inner concentric rings found on the 1964 models. The red-lined at 5300rpm tachometer was fitted to all 1965 Corvettes with the 300hp engine.

50. The steering wheel hub in 1965 Corvettes does not carry "Chevrolet Corvette" lettering as in 1964. A new electric clock with a 24 hour dial was added as was a four-way ignition switch.

51 & 52. Two views of a 1965 coupe fitted with 1967 wheels.

49

50

51

52

53

53. Corvettes of the 1963-67 era are strongly represented in contemporary club activities.

54. A 427cid-engined 1967 Corvette undergoing emergency surgery.

54

55

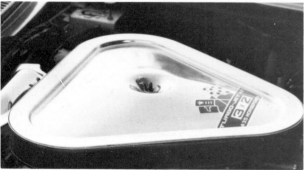

56

57

55. A 1967 convertible in a competitive stance.

56. Details of air-cleaner cover used on 1967 Corvettes with the 435hp, 427cid engine.

57. Rear window Peeping Tom's view of the 1967 coupe interior. The passenger side mounted fire extinguisher was a $14.95 option.

58. The 1967 seat pattern was unique to that year. The shoulder harness was optional and ordered on only 1426 Corvettes.

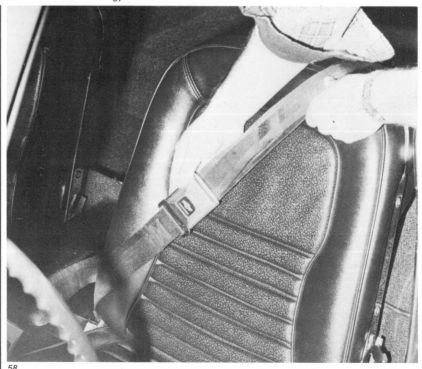

58

59. For ease of entry/exit the 1963-67 coupe doors were cut deeply into the roof section.

60 & 61. Three views of the hood and "cut away dome" fitted to all 1967 Corvettes equipped with a 427cid engine.

62. The N14 side mounted dual exhaust system was visually exciting but a bit too raucous for extended road use. Many Corvette owners have fitted contemporary tyres such as these Wide Tread GTs.

63. The final form of the 1963-67 side fender vents.

59

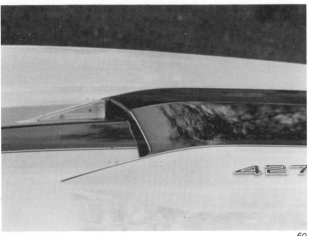

60

61

62

63

64. The rear deck script used on the 1967 model was unchanged from 1966.

65. This circular front parking-directional light design was used throughout the 1963-67 Corvette time span.

66. The 1967 Corvette fuel filler cap. The crossed flag background is body colour. The flags are larger and have a deeper angle than those of 1966. The circular "sun burst" has been eliminated.

67. A 1967 Corvette equipped with Turbo Hydramatic, 400hp/427cid V8 and optional off-road exhaust system. The raised section of the hood and scoop sections on 1967 Corvettes were colour keyed to the car's interior.

64

65

66

67

68. Exclusive to the 1967 Corvette were these ventilated steel wheels with a six-inch rim width.

69. The proposed, but never-built, four place Corvette.

68

69

70. An early (1960) proposal for the 1963 Corvette.

71. These pre-production Corvettes differed in many significant ways from the form finally adopted for 1963. Bill Mitchell's Sting Ray lurks in the background.

70

71

C1. Front fender (wing) details of 1964 Corvette Coupe. This standard wheel cover was used only on the 1964 models. Approximately 9,000 Corvettes used this polished steel type before a new version, with a frosted inner surface, was adopted.

C2. A totally original, documented 1964 Corvette Coupe with Tuxedo Black exterior, red interior and a total of 45,000 miles showing on the odometer. The only change made in this Coupe's as-delivered exterior appearance by its owners, Linda and Mike Strunk, was the replacement of its black wall tyres with white walls.

C1

C2

C3. The inside door knobs of the 1964 Corvette were chromed instead of having a black finish as found on the 1963 model. The twin safety reflectors were carried over from 1963.

C4. The carpeted luggage area of the 1964 Sport Coupe. Note the small "Air Conditioned" decal. The improved vision provided by the new one-piece rear window is evident.

C5. All 1964-66 Corvettes with the 327cid V8 had this front fender (wing)-mounted emblem which was slightly thicker than the item used in 1963.

C3

C4

C5

C6 & C7. 1964 Corvette Coupe. Note the distinctive change of appearance when the headlights are raised.

C6

C7

C8. The air cleaner of the 435hp/427cid engine carries a not-too-subtle notification of the 1967 Corvette's potency!

C9. The "Big Block" Corvette engines were built at Chevrolet's Tonawanda, New York, plant where it appears worker morale was quite high ...

C10. Details of the 1967 Corvette 435hp/427cid engine's triple carburetion. This engine was a $437.10 option.

C8

C9

C10

C11

C12

C11. By 1967 the Corvette was putting most sports cars in the shadow of its performance. Still, after a five-year production run, the Sting Ray Coupe remained an attractive and very contemporary sports car.

C12. Rear view of the 1967 Sting Ray Coupe. The radio antenna position is common to all 1963-67 Corvettes. The body-colour fuel filler cap was exclusive to the 1967 model.

C13. The raised dome and scoop of the 427-engined 1967 Corvettes combined with the windsplit hood design to create a dramatic appearance.

C14. Sting Ray coupes from 1964-67 had the single piece rear window. However vestiges of the original split window format remained in the form of the single rib running along the roof and extending into the rear deck.

C15. For 1965 the Corvette's seat pattern was changed from vertical to horizontal heat seams.

C16. Corvettes are often altered to suit the personal tastes of their owners. This 1965 convertible is a good example of a moderately modified Corvette.

C13

C14

C15

C16

C17. The area between the spokes of the Corvette's optional aluminium wheels was painted black in 1965. Previously an argent colour had been applied.

C18. 1965 was the only year Corvettes were available with the combination of fuel-injection and four-wheel disc brakes.

C19. A 1966 Coupe owner-modified to resemble the Grand Sport model of 1963.

C17

C18

C19

C20 & C21. Two views of the definitive 1963 Sting Ray Coupe, Tony Sofia's prize-winning, immaculately restored and maintained Z06 Coupe.

C20

C21